TABLE OF CONTENTS

COUNTRY OVERVIEW: TANZANIA AT A GLANCE

History

The history of Tanzania begins with the dawn of our species. Most experts agree that the earliest humans originated in fertile regions of East Africa. Cushitic-speaking people from southern Ethiopia migrated through the eastern part of the Great Rift Valley into north central Tanzania during the first millennium B.C. Early cattle herders found an unoccupied niche in the virgin grasslands and coexisted with the Khoisan hunters and gatherers who were already there. During the first millennium A.D., Bantu-speaking peoples originating from west central Africa filtered into western Tanzania and the fertile volcanic mountains of the northeast. These iron-working cultivators preferred wetter areas and thus avoided the dry savannas that were already occupied by hunters, gatherers and pastoralists.

Early residents of Tanzania's coastal region experienced heavy Eastern, rather than African, cultural influences, developing a different culture from the people living in the interior. Merchants from Egypt, Assyria, Phoenicia, Greece, India, Arabia, Persia, and China were already visiting this region during the first century A.D. By the ninth century, Arabs and Shirazi Persians were significant traders on the coast, and large numbers of them settled on the offshore islands. In time, the Arab and Shirazi communities intermingled with the Bantu-speaking mainland groups and a new culture — the Swahili — was born.

During the late 19th century, European explorers and missionaries used Zanzibar as a point of departure for the mainland. Their travels helped define future colonial boundaries and paved the way for Protestant and Roman Catholic missionaries.

In its desire to establish an economic and political foothold among other European powers, a newly unified Germany entered mainland Tanzania in 1884 and signed a series of agreements with local rulers that ceded administrative and commercial protection to Germany. With the onset of World War I, Germany lost control of mainland Tanzania. Great Britain took over and renamed the mainland Tanganyika. In 1922, the League of Nations consigned Tanganyika to the British Empire under its mandate system.

It was not until 1961 that Tanganyika gained independence from Britain, with Julius Nyerere serving as the country's first president. In January 1964, revolutionary forces overthrew the sultan of Zanzibar, and three months later, the mainland and the islands of Zanzibar joined to become the United Republic of Tanzania.

Government

The United Republic of Tanzania was formed on April 26, 1964, by the adoption of the Act of Union between Tanganyika and the islands of Zanzibar. The nation is governed under a Constitution formulated in 1977.

The chief executive of Tanzania is a president, currently Jakaya Kikwete, who is elected by popular vote to a five-year term. The president appoints a vice president, prime minister, and cabinet. Tanzania has a unicameral National Assembly with 244 members, 169 of whom are elected by popular vote to terms of five years. The rest of the members are elected by the National Assembly, are appointed by the president, or sit by virtue of being commissioners of the country's regions. The mainland is divided into 20 regions, Zanzibar's Unguja Island is divided into three regions, and Zanzibar's Pemba Island is split into two regions.

Economy

The economy of Tanzania is primarily agricultural. About 80 percent of the economically active population is engaged in farming, and agricultural products account for about 85 percent of annual exports. The country is the world's largest producer of cloves. Other products include tea, coffee, cashew nuts, sisal, timber, and cotton. In recent years, the mining industry has developed significantly, with gold, tanzanite, and diamonds providing jobs and income. The manufacturing sector is small and growing slowly.

With per capita income at an estimated $270 a year in 2002, Tanzania is one of the poorest countries in the world. Government programs once called for a form of socialism that kept people poor but relatively equal. Those policies were abandoned in the mid-1980s in favor of a free-enterprise system, which has generated more wealth, but also more disparity of income.

People and Culture

The population of Tanzania consists of more than 120 native African groups, the majority of whom speak a Bantu language. The largest groups are the Sukuma and the Nyamwezi, each representing about a fifth of the population. Tanzania is also home to people of Indian, Pakistani, and Goan origin, and small Arab and European communities.

The population of Tanzania is estimated to be close to 32 million, giving the country a population density of 106 people per square mile. The population distribution is irregular, with high densities in the fertile areas around Mount Kilimanjaro and the shores of Lake Victoria and comparatively low densities in much of the interior.

Muslims, Christians, and those with indigenous beliefs make up relatively equal proportions of Tanzania's population. Muslims live mainly along the coast and on Zanzibar, while Christians reside primarily inland and in the larger cities. Animist beliefs are still strong in many areas of the country.

Environment

The landscape of mainland Tanzania is generally flat along the coast, but a plateau with an average altitude of about 4,000 feet constitutes the majority of the country. Isolated mountain groups rise in the northeast and southwest. The volcanic Kilimanjaro (the highest mountain in Africa at 19,340 feet) is located near the northeastern border. Three of the great lakes of Africa lie on the Tanzanian border: Lake Victoria in the northwest, Lake Nyasa (also called Lake Malawi) in the southwest, and Lake Tanganyika in the west. The latter two rivers lie in the Great Rift Valley, a tremendous geological fault system that extends from the Middle East to Mozambique.

Zanzibar consists of the islands of Unguja and Pemba. Separated from the mainland by a channel that is approximately 25 miles wide, Unguja is about 55 miles long and covers an area of 640 square miles. It is the largest coral island off the coast of Africa. Pemba, some 25 miles northwest of Unguja, is about 42 miles long and has an area of 380 square miles.

Elevation and distance from the sea control the climate of Tanzania. The mainland coast along the Indian Ocean is warm and tropical, with temperatures averaging 80 degrees Fahrenheit and annual rainfall ranging from 30 to 55 inches. The inland plateau is hot and dry, with annual rainfall averaging as little as 20 inches. The semi-temperate highlands in the northeast and southwest receive more water and can get quite chilly.

RESOURCES FOR FURTHER INFORMATION

Following is a list of websites for additional information about the Peace Corps, Tanzania, and to connect you to returned Volunteers and other invitees. Please keep in mind that although we try to make sure all these links are active and current, we cannot guarantee it. If you do not have access to the Internet, visit your local library. Libraries offer free Internet usage and often let you print information to take home.

A note of caution: As you surf the Internet, be aware that you may find bulletin boards and chat rooms in which people are free to express opinions about the Peace Corps based on their own experience, including comments by those who were unhappy with their choice to serve in the Peace Corps. These opinions are not those of the Peace Corps or the U.S. government, and we hope you will keep in mind that no two people experience their service in the same way.

General Information About Tanzania

www.countrywatch.com

On this site, you can learn anything from what time it is in the capital of Tanzania to how to convert from the dollar to the Tanzania currency. Just click on Tanzania and go from there.

www.lonelyplanet.com/destinations

Visit this site for general travel advice about almost any country in the world.

www.state.gov

The State Department's website issues background notes periodically about countries around the world. Find Tanzania and learn more about its social and political history. You can also go to the site's international travel section to check on conditions that may affect your safety.

www.psr.keele.ac.uk/official.htm

This includes links to all the official sites for governments worldwide.

www.geography.about.com/library/maps/blindex.htm

This online world atlas includes maps and geographical information, and each country page contains links to other sites, such as the Library of Congress, that contain comprehensive historical, social, and political background.

www.cyberschoolbus.un.org/infonation/info.asp

This United Nations site allows you to search for statistical information for member states of the U.N.

www.worldinformation.com

This site provides an additional source of current and historical information about countries around the world.

Connect With Returned Volunteers and Other Invitees

www.rpcv.org

This is the site of the National Peace Corps Association, made up of returned Volunteers. On this site you can find links to all the Web pages of the "Friends of" groups for most countries of service, comprised of former Volunteers who served in those countries. There are also regional groups that frequently get together for social events and local volunteer activities. Or go straight to the Friends of Tanzania site: **www.fotanzania.org**

www.PeaceCorpsWorldwide.org

This site is hosted by a group of returned Volunteer writers. It is a monthly online publication of essays and Volunteer accounts of their Peace Corps service.

Online Articles/Current News Sites About Tanzania

www.ippmedia.com

News and radio from the Tanzanian perspective

www.theexpress.com

Site of a Tanzanian weekly published in English

International Development Sites About Tanzania

www.unaids.org

Thorough information on the AIDS epidemic from the Joint United Nations Programme on HIV/AIDS

www.usaid.gov/regions/afr/country_info/tanzania.html

An overview of the U.S. Agency for International Development's projects in Tanzania

Recommended Books

- Chinweizu (ed.). *Voices From Twentieth-Century Africa: Griots and Towncriers.* Boston: Faber and Faber, 1989.

- Fitzpatrick, Mary. *Lonely Planet: Tanzania.* Lonely Planet Publications, 2005.

- Maddox, Gregory, James L. Giblin, and Isaria N. Kimambo (eds.). *Custodians of the Land: Ecology and Culture in the History of Tanzania.* Athens: Ohio University Press, 1996.

- Pakenham, Thomas. *The Scramble for Africa: White Man's Conquest of the Dark Continent From 1876 to 1912.* New York: Random House, 1991.

- Yeager, Rodger. *Tanzania: An African Experiment* (2nd rev. ed.). San Francisco: Westview Press, 1991.

Books About the History of the Peace Corps

- Hoffman, Elizabeth Cobbs. *All You Need is Love: The Peace Corps and the Spirit of the 1960s.* Cambridge, Mass.: Harvard University Press, 2000.

- Rice, Gerald T. *The Bold Experiment: JFK's Peace Corps.* Notre Dame, Ind.: University of Notre Dame Press, 1985.

- Stossel, Scott. *Sarge: The Life and Times of Sargent Shriver.* Washington, D.C.: Smithsonian Institution Press, 2004.

- Meisler, Stanley. *When the World Calls: The Inside Story of the Peace Corps and its First 50 Years.* Boston, Mass.: Beacon Press, 2011.

Books on the Volunteer Experience

- Dirlam, Sharon. *Beyond Siberia: Two Years in a Forgotten Place.* Santa Barbara, Calif.: McSeas Books, 2004.

- Casebolt, Marjorie DeMoss. *Margarita: A Guatemalan Peace Corps Experience.* Gig Harbor, Wash.: Red Apple Publishing, 2000.

- Erdman, Sarah. Nine Hills to Nambonkaha: Two Years in the Heart of an African Village. New York, N.Y.: Picador, 2003.

- Hessler, Peter. *River Town: Two Years on the Yangtze.* New York, N.Y.: Perennial, 2001.

- Kennedy, Geraldine ed. *From the Center of the Earth: Stories out of the Peace Corps.* Santa Monica, Calif.: Clover Park Press, 1991.

- Thompsen, Moritz. *Living Poor: A Peace Corps Chronicle.* Seattle, Wash.: University of Washington Press, 1997 (reprint).

LIVING CONDITIONS AND VOLUNTEER LIFESTYLE

Communications
Mail

Few countries in the world offer the level of mail service considered normal in the United States. If you expect U.S. standards for mail service, you will be in for some frustration. Airmail can take up to a minimum of two weeks to arrive in Tanzania and sometimes can take two weeks or more to get to your site. Some mail may simply not arrive (fortunately, this is not a frequent occurrence, but it does happen). Advise your family and friends that mail delivery can be sporadic and they should not worry if they do not receive your letters regularly; also advise them to number their letters for tracking purposes and to include "Airmail" on envelopes.

Once you begin your Volunteer service, you can have mail sent directly to your site or to the Peace Corps office in Dar es Salaam. Education Volunteers often receive mail through their school's post office box, while other Volunteers usually rent a post office box in a nearby town. Most Volunteers find that their mail arrives faster when it goes directly to their site. During pre-service training, you will receive mail at the Peace Corps training site.

The address is:

"Your Name," PCT
Peace Corps Training Site
PO Box 9123
Dar es Salaam, Tanzania

Packages sent via surface mail normally take three to six months to reach Tanzania from the United States. Packages sent by air take from three to eight weeks. Hefty duty fees may be imposed on certain items. Although Volunteers can have packages sent to the Peace Corps office in Dar es Salaam, you are strongly advised to have them sent directly to your site. For your first six months of service, Peace Corps/Tanzania will pay the cost of clearing one package through customs and forwarding it to you at your site (a maximum of 15,000 shillings, or about $15). After that, with few exceptions, Peace Corps will not clear additional packages for you unless there is a firm work-related reason for the shipment that has been pre-approved by your supervisor. We recommend you wait to have packages sent until you get to your site and know what you really want or need.

Telephones

Most large cities, regional capitals, and many smaller towns have domestic long-distance service, while regional capitals and all large cities have overseas service. Most Volunteers have cellphones (which should be purchased in Tanzania to ensure compatibility with local cellphone services) and find text messaging friends and the office in-country to be a fast, reliable, and inexpensive way to communicate.

Because long-distance phone service is expensive, we recommend you have friends and family call from the United States rather than placing calls yourself. Because it sometimes takes several hours (on either end) to get a call through, you should not plan on regular phone calls as the primary means of communication with loved ones back home.

Computer, Internet, and Email Access

Environment Volunteers are discouraged from bringing personal computers to Tanzania as their sites seldom have electricity. Many education and school health Volunteer sites have electricity, so a laptop computer can be a convenience, but is certainly not a necessity. Limited repair facilities, the potential for theft, and fluctuating electrical currents make for short computer life spans. Most Volunteers do not bring computers to Tanzania.

Access to the Internet, e-mail, and word processing is common in larger cites and becoming increasingly available in towns nationwide. Computers with Microsoft Word and Excel, as well as limited Internet access, are available at the Peace Corps office in Dar es Salaam.

Most Volunteers can access e-mail at least once a month, though a Volunteer may, on occasion, travel to a nearby town and find the network is not functioning.

Housing and Site Location

Volunteer sites range from towns in the North near Mount Kilimanjaro to Songea in the South. No Volunteers serve along the western borders with Uganda, Burundi, Rwanda, or Lake Tanganyika and Victoria. Health Volunteers are assigned to communities where there are primary and secondary schools and a health center. Education Volunteers are posted at or near secondary schools in both rural and urban sites, while environment Volunteers work in village communities. The determination of a Volunteer's site is made during training, after staff members have had an opportunity to match an individual's strengths and capabilities with the needs of the host community or school.

Volunteer housing, which is usually similar to that of Tanzanians living in the same community, is generally modest but comfortable. Housing varies in size, but all houses are made of either cement block or fired brick with tin or tile roofs. Houses have at least two rooms and are sometimes furnished with a bed, a table, chairs, and possibly other items. Volunteers receive a settling-in allowance to assist them in obtaining basic household items and in purchasing a cell phone. Volunteer sites are located anywhere from a few hours to a few days from Dar es Salaam. Proximity to the nearest fellow Peace Corps Volunteer varies from site to site. Your nearest expatriate neighbor might be a British (Voluntary Service

Overseas, or VSO) or Japanese (Japanese International Cooperation Agency, or JICA) volunteer.

Volunteers generally are placed alone and live alone, although having two Volunteers at one site or even in one house or sharing housing with a host country national is a possibility. The phrase "live alone" may be misleading, however. Tanzania has a collectivist or group-based culture, which means American concepts of privacy and personal space are neither understood, nor always respected. Neighborhood children will be in and out of your house on a regular basis, and adult neighbors and colleagues will be part of your daily life.

Some Volunteers have electricity and running water, but the quality and reliability of both are often poor. These services become scarcer as sites become more rural; in these areas, water may come from a community well or river, and evening light is often limited to candles and lanterns. Whatever the circumstances, it is important you remain flexible while you adjust to your new lifestyle.

Living Allowance and Money Management

As a Volunteer, you will receive a modest but sufficient living allowance, paid in Tanzania shillings that will allow you to live at the same economic level as your Tanzanian colleagues. Nevertheless, in many cases, your remuneration will be greater than your counterpart's or supervisor's salary. The amount of this allowance is based on regular surveys of Volunteers and the cost of living in Tanzania and is intended to cover food, utilities, household supplies, clothing, recreation and entertainment, transportation, reading materials, and other incidentals. The living allowance (currently equivalent to about $180 per month) is paid bi-monthly into Volunteers' local bank accounts, so your ability to manage funds wisely is important.

You will also receive a settling-in allowance, which includes funds to purchase a cell phone, basic household furnishings, kitchen equipment, linens and other items to make your new house a home. The Peace Corps will also provide bicycles to Volunteers who want them. A helmet (provided by the Peace Corps) must be worn at all times when riding your bicycle. Finally, you will receive a leave allowance of $24 per month (standard in all Peace Corps countries), paid in local currency with your living allowance.

Volunteers suggest you bring cash or credit cards for vacation travel. Credit cards are accepted only at the more expensive tourist destinations, but it is possible to get cash advances via credit cards (for a fee) in Arusha and Dar es Salaam. However, keep in mind that credit card fraud is a significant problem in Tanzania. Most stores and hotels will only accept Visa card. Volunteers who rely on MasterCard may struggle to find places to use them.

Food and Diet

The staple food in Tanzania is maize (corn), which is prepared as a thick porridge called ugali and eaten with vegetables or beans. Meat and chicken are almost always available, and fish is plentiful in the coastal and lake areas. Many fruits and vegetables grow in Tanzania (though not all items are available year-round), and with a little creativity, you should be able to enjoy a varied diet. Most Volunteers prepare their own food, although after becoming more familiar with their sites, some Volunteers hire someone to help with household work, including cooking.

Volunteers who are vegetarian will be able to eat well in Tanzania after becoming familiar with local foods and their preparation. Vegans may have to be flexible to meet their nutritional needs. Most Tanzanians are not familiar with vegetarianism and normally will not be prepared to serve a vegetarian meal if you are a guest in their home. (It is a sign of good hospitality to serve meat to one's guests.) Volunteers who are vegetarians will often be asked why they do not eat meat. Every Volunteer has a different way of answering this question. Some simply say they do not like meat; some say their religion has rules about meat (whether that is true or not); and some say they choose not to eat meat for health reasons. In any case, a sensitive explanation of your dietary preferences is likely to be accepted.

One former Volunteer offers this advice on handling situations involving food: "When a Volunteer is offered some food or drink they do not like, they will often refuse it and say they do not want anything, or may claim they are not hungry or thirsty. Try to find something you will eat or drink and thank them for it. If you do not like beer or soda, maybe have some tea. If you do not like meat, have some beans or potatoes. You cannot simply refuse everything — they will not stop asking until you accept something from them. Enjoy what you can, and be polite and gracious for what you cannot tolerate."

Transportation

Volunteers' primary mode of long-distance transport is public buses. For shorter excursions, Volunteers use a daladala or a bicycle. A daladala is a minibus or small pickup truck that carries people and goods. (Yes, chickens could end up in your lap!) Buses and daladalas travel between or within towns on irregular schedules (i.e., when full), so travel in Tanzania is never a predictable affair. Many Volunteers find that in-country travel options are one of the biggest difficulties they encounter. While there are more buses available every year, this can make roads even more crowded and dangerous for travel.

Geography and Climate

Tanzania, located in southeastern Africa, borders Kenya and Uganda to the north; the Indian Ocean to the east; Mozambique, Malawi, and Zambia to the south; and Zaire, Burundi, and Rwanda to the west. The country includes the islands of Zanzibar in the

Indian Ocean. The total area of Tanzania is 378,035 square miles (945,087 square kilometers).

Because the country is south of the equator, the seasons will be opposite of what you are accustomed to. In June, July, and August (the cold season), temperatures range from 60 to 75 degrees Fahrenheit in the lowlands and on the coast to 40 to 50 degrees in the highlands. The hottest months of the year are November, December, and January when temperatures in the highlands range from 70 to 80 degrees and those in the lowlands range from 90 to 105 degrees, with considerable humidity. The rainy season starts in late November or early December and continues through April. The rest of the year is dry, but many highland areas have showers and mist year-round. A jacket or fleece top is recommended for the cool season, and loose-fitting cotton clothes are recommended for the hot season.

The landscape of Tanzania is quite diverse. The north is home to Mount Kilimanjaro, the highest point on the African continent, as well as Mount Meru and Hanang, the third and fifth highest points in East Africa, respectively. The north is also home to numerous game parks, including the Serengeti Plain and Ngorongoro Crater, a World Heritage site. The surrounding areas in the Great Rift Valley are also popular tourist destinations.

Tanzania contains or borders several important lakes. Lake Manyara and Lake Natron in the northern interior feature great migrations of flamingos and stunning scenery. On the northern border is Lake Victoria, the mouth of the White Nile River and the location of major commercial fishing operations. To the west lie Lake Tanganyika and, farther south, Lake Nyasa (also called Lake Malawi).

Social Activities

Larger towns often have discos and bars, which can become very lively on both weekdays and weekends. The most common form of entertainment is socializing with friends and neighbors. Some Volunteers visit other Volunteers on weekends and holidays. Although we encourage Volunteers to remain at their sites as much as possible in order to develop relationships with people in their community, we recognize that an occasional trip to the capital or to visit friends is important as well.

Tanzania has several television stations that broadcast nationwide. These stations have limited programming, but they offer a few programs from South Africa, the United States, and Europe. Satellite television is available in many cities. Tanzanian radio is quite good if you are in an area that receives FM broadcasts. Volunteers placed in rural areas rely on shortwave radio broadcasts from the BBC, Voice of America, or Radio Deutsche Wella. There is one modern cinema in Dar es Salaam, and some hotels and bars show videos of American or European films.

Professionalism, Dress, and Behavior

Norms for dress are much more conservative in Tanzania than in the United States. In the United States, many of us view our clothes as a reflection of our individuality; in Tanzania, people view one's dress as a sign of respect for others. Tanzanians do not appreciate clothes that are dirty, have holes in them, or are too revealing or too casual. Wearing such clothes will reduce both the amount of respect you gain and your effectiveness at work. While some of your counterparts may dress in seemingly worn or shabby clothes, this will be due to economics rather than choice. The likelihood is that they are wearing their best. A foreigner who wears ragged, unmended clothing, however, is likely to be considered an affront.

Although considered fashionable in the United States, accessories like nose and tongue rings and earrings on men are frowned upon in Tanzania. This is particularly true in rural areas. Volunteers who accessorize in this way may encounter negative feelings or feedback from the people with whom they live and work. This might be because they think you are gay (homosexuality is not widely accepted in Tanzania) or because they think you are unprofessionally dressed.

Whether you work as a teacher, health educator, or environmentalist, you will be perceived as a high-status professional. You will be "on duty" seven days a week, 24 hours a day and need to make every effort to conform to the behavior and dress expected of educated and high-status people in your school or community. One of the difficulties of finding your place as a Peace Corps Volunteer is fitting into the local culture while maintaining your own cultural identity and acting like a professional at the same time. It is not always an easy situation to resolve, but the Peace Corps will provide you with guidelines and recommendations.

Working effectively in another culture requires a certain level of sacrifice and flexibility that can be difficult for some people. The Peace Corps expects Volunteers to behave in a manner that will foster respect within their community or school and reflect well on the Peace Corps. Behavior that jeopardizes the Peace Corps program or your personal safety cannot be tolerated and could lead to administrative separation — a decision by the Peace Corps to terminate your service. If you have reservations about your ability or willingness to make these accommodations, you should reevaluate your decision to become a Volunteer.

Personal Safety

More detailed information about the Peace Corps' approach to safety is contained in the "Health Care and Safety" chapter, but it is an important issue and cannot be overemphasized. As stated in the Volunteer Handbook, becoming a Peace Corps Volunteer entails certain safety risks. Living and traveling in an unfamiliar environment (oftentimes alone), having a limited understanding of local language and culture, and being perceived as well-off are some of the factors that can put a Volunteer at risk. Many Volunteers experience varying degrees of unwanted attention and harassment. Petty thefts and burglaries are not uncommon, and incidents of physical and sexual assault do occur, although most Tanzania Volunteers complete their two years of service without incident. The Peace Corps has established procedures and policies designed to help you reduce your risks and enhance your safety and security. These procedures and policies, in addition to safety training, will be provided once you arrive in Tanzania. Using these tools, you are expected to take responsibility for your safety and well-being.

Each staff member at the Peace Corps is committed to providing Volunteers with the support they need to successfully meet the challenges they will face to have a safe, healthy, and productive service. We encourage Volunteers and families to look at our safety and security information on the Peace Corps website at **www.peacecorps.gov/safety**.

Information on these pages gives messages on Volunteer health and Volunteer safety. There is a section titled "Safety and Security – Our Partnership." Among topics addressed are the risks of serving as a Volunteer, posts' safety support systems, and emergency planning and communications.

Rewards and Frustrations

Although the potential for job satisfaction in Tanzania is very high, like all Volunteers, you may encounter frustrations. Perceptions of time, status, privacy, protocol, and efficiency are often very different from those in America. The lack of basic infrastructure can be challenging, and host agencies do not always provide expected support in a timely manner.

Tanzanians' views of Americans often come from the television shows, movies, or pop stars they see or hear. They generally perceive Americans as being very rich, so you are likely to be asked for money on a regular basis. The way American women behave and are treated in our culture is also an area of considerable curiosity and surprise to Tanzanians. Confronting these issues is part of what makes the Peace Corps experience so special. Although bridging cross-cultural differences will potentially be the hardest thing you ever do, it is also likely to be one of the most fulfilling.

It is a special time to be a Peace Corps Volunteer in Tanzania. With the devastating AIDS epidemic dramatically affecting all sectors of Tanzanian society, your efforts in working with youth and community members will be more important than at any other time in Peace Corps/Tanzania's history. You will be given a great deal of responsibility and independence in your work — perhaps more than in any other job you have had or will have. You will often need to motivate yourself and others with little guidance from supervisors. You might work for months without seeing any visible impact from, or without receiving feedback on, your work. Development is a slow process. You must possess the self-confidence, patience, and vision to continue working toward long-term goals without seeing immediate results. Nevertheless, most Volunteers leave Tanzania feeling they have gained much more than they sacrificed during their service. If you are able to make the commitment to integrate into your community and work hard, your service is sure to be a life-altering experience.

PEACE CORPS TRAINING

Pre-Service Training

Training is an essential part of Peace Corps service. Learning to live and work in a new culture and environment can be quite challenging. The goal of pre-service training is to give you enough skills and information to allow you to live and work effectively in Tanzania.

The five major components of training are technical skills, cross-cultural adaptation, language, personal health, and safety and security, which are presented in an integrated manner. You will live with a Tanzanian family and interact daily with Tanzanians during most of your training. You will also have opportunities to work with and learn from Tanzanians in real-life experiences. Education Volunteers will spend three weeks at an internship school near their host family's home. Environmental Volunteers will have the opportunity to learn directly from farmers in the villages where their training takes place. Health Volunteers will be able to gain valuable experience in schools and health facilities near their training site. The training period can be both stressful and exhilarating. You will confront a new culture, work to gain fluency in a new language, learn new professional skills, and build support systems with others who are going through the same roller-coaster of adjustments. You will need patience, flexibility, energy, and good humor to get the most out of this rich experience. You will find the Peace Corps' training staff ready and willing to accommodate your needs and help you get off to the best possible start. The Peace Corps anticipates that you will approach training with an open mind, a desire to learn, and a willingness to become involved.

Technical Training

Technical training will prepare you to work in Tanzania by building on the skills you already have and helping you develop new skills in a manner appropriate to the needs of the country. The Peace Corps staff, Tanzania experts, and current Volunteers will conduct the training program. Training places great emphasis on learning how to transfer the skills you have to the community in which you will serve as a Volunteer.

Technical training will include sessions on the general economic and political environment in Tanzania and strategies for working within such a framework. You will review your technical sector's goals and will meet with the Tanzania agencies and organizations that invited the Peace Corps to assist them. You will be supported and evaluated throughout the training to build the confidence and skills you need to undertake your project activities and be a productive member of your community.

Language Training

As a Peace Corps Volunteer, you will find that language skills are key to personal and professional satisfaction during your service. These skills are critical to your job performance, they help you integrate into your community, and they can ease your personal adaptation to the new surroundings. Therefore, language training is at the heart of the training program. You must successfully meet minimum language requirements to complete training and become a Volunteer. Tanzania language instructors teach formal language classes five days a week in small groups of four to five people.

Your language training will incorporate a community-based approach. In addition to classroom time, you will be given assignments to work on outside of the classroom and with your host family. The goal is to get you to a point of basic social communication skills so you can practice and develop language skills further once you are at your site. Prior to being sworn in as a Volunteer, you will work on strategies to continue language studies during your service.

Cross-Cultural Training

As part of your pre-service training, you will live with a Tanzania host family. This experience is designed to ease your transition to life at your site. Families go through an orientation conducted by Peace Corps staff to explain the purpose of pre-service training and to assist them in helping you adapt to living in Tanzania. Many Volunteers form strong and lasting friendships with their host families.

Cross-cultural and community development training will help you improve your communication skills and understand your role as a facilitator of development. You will be exposed to topics such as community mobilization, conflict resolution, gender and development, nonformal and adult education strategies, and political structures.

Health Training

During pre-service training, you will be given basic medical training and information. You will be expected to practice preventive health care and to take responsibility for your own health by adhering to all medical policies. Trainees are required to attend all medical sessions. The topics include preventive health measures and minor and major medical issues that you might encounter while in Tanzania. Nutrition, mental health, setting up a safe living compound, and how to avoid HIV/AIDS and other sexually transmitted diseases (STDs) are also covered.

Safety Training

During the safety training sessions, you will learn how to adopt a lifestyle that reduces your risks at home, at work, and during your travels. You will also learn appropriate, effective strategies for coping with unwanted attention and about your individual responsibility for promoting safety throughout your service.

Additional Trainings During Volunteer Service

In its commitment to institutionalize quality training, the Peace Corps has implemented a training system that provides Volunteers with continual opportunities to examine their commitment to Peace Corps service while increasing their technical and cross-cultural skills. During service, there are usually three training events. The titles and objectives for those trainings are as follows:

- In-service training: Provides an opportunity for Volunteers to upgrade their technical, language, and project development skills while sharing their experiences and reaffirming their commitment after having served for three to six months.

- Midterm conference (done in conjunction with technical sector in-service): Assists Volunteers in reviewing their first year, reassessing their personal and project objectives, and planning for their second year of service.

- Close-of-service conference: Prepares Volunteers for the future after Peace Corps service and reviews their respective projects and personal experiences.

The number, length, and design of these trainings are adapted to country-specific needs and conditions. The key to the training system is that training events are integrated and interrelated, from the pre-departure orientation through the end of your service, and are planned, implemented, and evaluated cooperatively by the training staff, Peace Corps staff, and Volunteers.

YOUR HEALTH CARE AND
SAFETY IN TANZANIA

The Peace Corps' highest priority is maintaining the good health and safety of every Volunteer. Peace Corps medical programs emphasize the preventive, rather than the curative, approach to disease. The Peace Corps in Tanzania maintains a clinic with a full-time medical officer, who takes care of Volunteers' primary health care needs. Additional medical services, such as testing and basic treatment, are also available in Tanzania at local hospitals. If you become seriously ill, you will be transported either to an American-standard medical facility in the region or to the United States.

Health Issues in Tanzania

The most common health problems in Tanzania are ones that also exist in the United States, such as colds, diarrhea, skin infections, headaches, minor injuries, sexually transmitted diseases, and adjustment disorders. These problems may be more frequent or compounded by life in Tanzania because environmental factors in-country raise the risk of, or exacerbate the severity of, certain illnesses and injuries.

Illnesses specific to Tanzania are those typical of other tropical countries, such as malaria, schistosomiasis, gastrointestinal disorders, typhoid fever, and hepatitis. All of these are preventable with appropriate knowledge and interventions. You will be vaccinated in-country against hepatitis A and B, meningitis, tetanus, typhoid, and rabies. Because malaria is endemic in Tanzania, taking antimalarial medication is required of all Volunteers. If you do not want to take malaria prophylaxis, you should not come to Tanzania.

Tanzania is one of the countries most affected by the HIV/AIDS pandemic, which can impact anyone, males and females, adults and children, regardless of sexual orientation. You will receive more information from the medical officer about this important issue.

Alcohol is an integral part of many social interactions in Tanzania, and you may feel pressure to drink in these situations. If you have any problem with the use of alcohol, be sure that you can manage this type of pressure before accepting an assignment in Tanzania. Currently, Alcoholics Anonymous meetings exist only in the capital and Arusha.

Helping You Stay Healthy

The Peace Corps will provide you with all the necessary inoculations, medications, and information to stay healthy. Upon your arrival in Tanzania, you will receive a medical handbook. At the end of training, you will receive a medical kit with supplies to take care of mild illnesses and first aid needs. The contents of the kit are listed later in this chapter.

During pre-service training, you will have access to basic medical supplies through the medical officer. However, you will be responsible for your own supply of prescription drugs and any other specific medical supplies you require, as the Peace Corps will not order these items during training. Please bring a three-month supply of any prescription drugs you use, since they may not be available here and it may take several months for shipments to arrive.

You will have physicals at midservice and at the end of your service. If you develop a serious medical problem during your service, the medical officer in Tanzania will consult with the Office of Medical Services in Washington, D.C. If it is determined that your condition cannot be treated in Tanzania, you may be sent out of the country for further evaluation and care.

Maintaining Your Health

As a Volunteer, you must accept considerable responsibility for your own health. Proper precautions will significantly reduce your risk of serious illness or injury. The adage "An ounce of prevention ..." becomes extremely important in areas where diagnostic and treatment facilities are not up to the standards of the United States. The most important of your responsibilities in Tanzania is to take the following preventive measures:

Malaria is endemic in most of Tanzania and is present throughout the year. The disease can kill you if left untreated, so prevention and early recognition of infection are extremely important. It is mandatory that you take malaria prophylaxis, and other preventive measures (such as sleeping under a mosquito net) are strongly encouraged. You will learn how to make a blood slide diagnosis and how to treat malaria if you become infected.

Schistosomiasis is a parasitic infection that can be contracted by swimming or wading in infected water. Lake Victoria and most other freshwater bodies in the country harbor the parasite. Symptoms can take time to develop, so the Peace Corps routinely screens for the infection at the end of Volunteer service.

Many illnesses that afflict Volunteers worldwide are entirely preventable if proper food and water precautions are taken. These illnesses include food poisoning, parasitic infections, hepatitis A, dysentery, Guinea worms, tapeworms, and typhoid fever. Your medical officer will discuss specific standards for water and food preparation in Tanzania during pre-service training.

Abstinence is the only certain choice for preventing infection with HIV and other sexually transmitted diseases. You are taking risks if you choose to be sexually active. To lessen risk, use a condom every time you have sex. Whether your partner is a host country citizen, a fellow Volunteer, or anyone else, do not assume this person is free of HIV/AIDS or other STDs. You will receive more information from the medical officer about this important issue.

Volunteers are expected to adhere to an effective means of birth control to prevent an unplanned pregnancy. Your medical officer can help you decide on the most appropriate method to suit your individual needs. Contraceptive methods are available without charge from the medical officer.

It is critical to your health that you promptly report to the medical office or other designated facility for scheduled immunizations, and that you let the medical officer know immediately of significant illnesses and injuries.

Women's Health Information

Pregnancy is treated in the same manner as other Volunteer health conditions that require medical attention but also have programmatic ramifications. The Peace Corps is responsible for determining the medical risk and the availability of appropriate medical care if the Volunteer remains in-country. Given the circumstances under which Volunteers live and work in Peace Corps countries, it is rare that the Peace Corps' medical and programmatic standards for continued service during pregnancy can be met.

If feminine hygiene products are not available for you to purchase on the local market, the Peace Corps medical officer in Tanzania will provide them. If you require a specific product, please bring a three-month supply with you.

Your Peace Corps Medical Kit

The Peace Corps medical officer will provide you with a kit that contains basic items necessary to prevent and treat illnesses that may occur during service. Kit items can be periodically restocked at the medical office.

Medical Kit Contents

Ace bandages
Adhesive tape
American Red Cross First Aid & Safety
    Handbook
Antacid tablets (Tums)
Antibiotic ointment (Bacitracin/Neomycin/
    Polymycin B)
Antiseptic antimicrobial skin cleaner
    (Hibiclens)
Band-Aids
Butterfly closures
Calamine lotion
Cepacol lozenges
Condoms

Dental floss
Diphenhydramine HCL 25 mg (Benadryl)
Insect repellent stick (Cutter's)
Iodine tablets (for water purification)
Lip balm (Chapstick)
Oral rehydration salts
Oral thermometer (Fahrenheit)
Pseudoephedrine HCL 30 mg (Sudafed)
Robitussin-DM lozenges (for cough)
Scissors
Sterile gauze pads
Tetrahydrozaline eyedrops (Visine)
Tinactin (antifungal cream)
Tweezers

Before You Leave: A Medical Checklist

If there has been any change in your health – physical, mental, or dental – since you submitted your examination reports to the Peace Corps, you must immediately notify the Office of Medical Services. Failure to disclose new illnesses, injuries, allergies, or pregnancy can endanger your health and may jeopardize your eligibility to serve.

If your dental exam was done more than a year ago, or if your physical exam is more than two years old, contact the Office of Medical Services to find out whether you need to update your records. If your dentist or Peace Corps dental consultant has recommended that you undergo dental treatment or repair, you must complete that work and make sure your dentist sends requested confirmation reports or X-rays to the Office of Medical Services.

If you wish to avoid having duplicate vaccinations, contact your physician's office to obtain a copy of your immunization record and bring it to your pre-departure orientation. If you have any immunizations prior to Peace Corps service, the Peace Corps cannot reimburse you for the cost. The Peace Corps will provide all the immunizations necessary for your overseas assignment, either at your pre-departure orientation or shortly after you arrive in Tanzania. You do not need to begin taking malaria medication prior to departure.

Bring a three-month supply of any prescription or over-the-counter medication you use on a regular basis, including birth control pills. Although the Peace Corps cannot reimburse you for this three-month supply, it will order refills during your service. While awaiting shipment – which can take several months – you will be dependent on your own medication supply. The Peace Corps will not pay for herbal or nonprescribed medications, such as St. John's wort, glucosamine, selenium, or antioxidant supplements.

You are encouraged to bring copies of medical prescriptions signed by your physician. This is not a requirement, but they might come in handy if you are questioned in transit about carrying a three-month supply of prescription drugs.

If you wear eyeglasses, bring two pairs with you – a pair and a spare. If a pair breaks, the Peace Corps will replace them, using the information your doctor in the United States provided on the eyeglasses form during your examination. The Peace Corps discourages you from using contact lenses during your service to reduce your risk of developing a serious infection or other eye disease. Most Peace Corps countries do not have appropriate water and sanitation to support eye care with the use of contact lenses. The Peace Corps will not supply or replace contact lenses or associated solutions unless an ophthalmologist has recommended their use for a specific medical condition and the Peace Corps' Office of Medical Services has given approval.

If you are eligible for Medicare, are over 50 years of age, or have a health condition that may restrict your future participation in health care plans, you may wish to consult an insurance specialist about unique coverage needs before your departure. The Peace Corps will provide all necessary health care from the time you leave for your pre-departure orientation until you complete your service. When you finish, you will be entitled to the post-service health care benefits described in the Peace Corps Volunteer Handbook. You may wish to consider keeping an existing health plan in effect during your service if you think age or pre-existing conditions might prevent you from re-enrolling in your current plan when you return home.

SAFETY AND SECURITY: OUR PARTNERSHIP

Serving as a Volunteer overseas entails certain safety and security risks. Living and traveling in an unfamiliar environment, a limited understanding of the local language and culture, and the perception of being a wealthy American are some of the factors that can put a Volunteer at risk. Property theft and burglaries are not uncommon. Incidents of physical and sexual assault do occur, although almost all Volunteers complete their two years of service without serious personal safety problems.

Beyond knowing that Peace Corps approaches safety and security as a partnership with you, it might be helpful to see how this partnership works. Peace Corps has policies, procedures, and training in place to promote your safety. We depend on you to follow those policies and to put into practice what you have learned. An example of how this works in practice – in this case to help manage the risk of burglary – is:

- Peace Corps assesses the security environment where you will live and work
- Peace Corps inspects the house where you will live according to established security criteria
- Peace Corps provides you with resources to take measures such as installing new locks
- Peace Corps ensures you are welcomed by host country authorities in your new community
- Peace Corps responds to security concerns that you raise
- You lock your doors and windows
- You adopt a lifestyle appropriate to the community where you live
- You get to know neighbors
- You decide if purchasing personal articles insurance is appropriate for you
- You don't change residences before being authorized by Peace Corps
- You communicate concerns that you have to Peace Corps staff

Factors that Contribute to Volunteer Risk

There are several factors that can heighten a Volunteer's risk, many of which are within the Volunteer's control. By far the most common crime that Volunteers experience is theft. Thefts often occur when Volunteers are away from their sites, in crowded locations (such as markets or on public transportation), and when leaving items unattended.

Before you depart for Tanzania there are several measures you can take to reduce your risk:

- Leave valuable objects in the U.S.

- Leave copies of important documents and account numbers with someone you trust in the U.S.

- Purchase a hidden money pouch or "dummy" wallet as a decoy

- Purchase personal articles insurance

After you arrive in Tanzania, you will receive more detailed information about common crimes, factors that contribute to Volunteer risk, and local strategies to reduce that risk. For example, Volunteers in Tanzania learn to:

- Choose safe routes and times for travel, and travel with someone trusted by the community whenever possible

- Make sure one's personal appearance is respectful of local customs

- Avoid high-crime areas

- Know the local language to get help in an emergency

- Make friends with local people who are respected in the community

- Limit alcohol consumption

As you can see from this list, you must be willing to work hard and adapt your lifestyle to minimize the potential for being a target for crime. As with anywhere in the world, crime does exist in Tanzania. You can reduce your risk by avoiding situations that place you at risk and by taking precautions. Crime at the village or town level is less frequent than in the large cities; people know each other and generally are less likely to steal from their neighbors. Tourist attractions in large towns are favorite worksites for pickpockets.

The following are other security concerns in Tanzania of which you should be aware:

When it comes to your safety and security in the Peace Corps, you have to be willing to adapt your behavior and lifestyle to minimize the potential for being a target for crime. As with anywhere in the world, crime does exist in Tanzania. You can reduce your risk by avoiding situations that make you feel uncomfortable and by taking precautions. Crime at the village or town level is less frequent than in the large cities; people know each other and generally will not steal from their neighbors. Tourist attractions in large towns, for instance, are favorite work sites for pickpockets. The following are safety concerns in Tanzania of which you should be aware:

In Dar es Salaam and Arusha, Tanzania's two largest cities, there are certain areas where robberies and muggings are more frequent. These will be pointed out to you, and you will be advised either to avoid walking in these areas altogether or to walk there only in a group.

Modes of public transport, including buses and boats, are often in poor condition and overcrowded, and they generally travel at unsafe speeds. In addition, many roads are in disrepair. When taking public transport, it is important to use common sense, avoid traveling at night, and be careful with your valuables.

While whistles and exclamations may be fairly common on the street, this behavior can be reduced if you dress conservatively, abide by local cultural norms, and respond according to the training you will receive.

Staying Safe: Don't Be a Target for Crime

You must be prepared to take on a large degree of responsibility for your own safety. You can make yourself less of a target, ensure that your home is secure, and develop relationships in your community that will make you an unlikely victim of crime. While the factors that contribute to your risk in Tanzania may be different, in many ways you can do what you would do if you moved to a new city anywhere: Be cautious, check things out, ask questions, learn about your neighborhood, know where the more risky locations are, use common sense, and be aware. You can reduce your vulnerability to crime by integrating into your community, learning the local language, acting responsibly, and abiding by Peace Corps policies and procedures. Serving safely and effectively in Tanzania will require that you accept some restrictions on your current lifestyle.

Support from Staff

If a trainee or Volunteer is the victim of a safety incident, Peace Corps staff is prepared to provide support. All Peace Corps posts have procedures in place to respond to incidents of crime committed against Volunteers. The first priority for all posts in the aftermath of an incident is to ensure the Volunteer is safe and receiving medical treatment as needed. After assuring the safety of the Volunteer, Peace Corps staff response may include reassessing the Volunteer's worksite and housing arrangements and making any adjustments, as needed. In some cases, the nature of the incident may necessitate a site or housing transfer. Peace Corps staff will also assist Volunteers with preserving their rights to pursue legal sanctions against the perpetrators of the crime. It is very important that Volunteers report incidents as they occur, not only to protect their peer Volunteers, but also to preserve the future right to prosecute. Should Volunteers decide later in the process that they want to proceed with the prosecution of their assailant, this option may no longer exist if the evidence of the event has not been preserved at the time of the incident.

Crime Data for Tanzania

Crime data and statistics for Tanzania, which is updated yearly, are available at the following link: **http://www.peacecorps.gov/countrydata/tanzania**

Please take the time to review this important information.

Few Peace Corps Volunteers are victims of serious crimes and crimes that do occur overseas are investigated and prosecuted by local authorities through the local courts system. If you are the victim of a crime, you will decide if you wish to pursue prosecution. If you decide to prosecute, Peace Corps will be there to assist you. One of our tasks is to ensure you are fully informed of your options and understand how the local legal process works. Peace Corps will help you ensure your rights are protected to the fullest extent possible under the laws of the country.

If you are the victim of a serious crime, you will learn how to get to a safe location as quickly as possible and contact your Peace Corps office. It's important that you notify Peace Corps as soon as you can so Peace Corps can provide you with the help you need.

Volunteer Safety Support in Tanzania

The Peace Corps' approach to safety is a five-pronged plan to help you stay safe during your service and includes the following: information sharing, Volunteer training, site selection criteria, a detailed emergency action plan, and protocols for addressing safety and security incidents. Tanzania's in-country safety program is outlined below.

The Peace Corps/Tanzania office will keep you informed of any issues that may impact Volunteer safety through **information sharing**. Regular updates will be provided in Volunteer newsletters and in memorandums from the country director. In the event of a critical situation or emergency, you will be contacted through the emergency communication network. An important component of the capacity of Peace Corps to keep you informed is your buy-in to the partnership concept with the Peace Corps staff. It is expected that you will do your part in ensuring that Peace Corps staff members are kept apprised of your movements in-country so they are able to inform you.

Volunteer training will include sessions on specific safety and security issues in Tanzania. This training will prepare you to adopt a culturally appropriate lifestyle and exercise judgment that promotes safety and reduces risk in your home, at work, and while traveling. Safety training is offered throughout service and is integrated into the language, cross-cultural aspects, health, and other components of training. You will be expected to successfully complete all training competencies in a variety of areas, including safety and security, as a condition of service.

Certain **site selection criteria** are used to determine safe housing for Volunteers before their arrival. The Peace Corps staff works closely with host communities and counterpart agencies to help prepare them for a Volunteer's arrival and to establish expectations of their respective roles in supporting the Volunteer. Each site is inspected before the Volunteer's arrival to ensure placement in appropriate, safe, and secure housing and worksites. Site selection is based, in part, on any relevant site history; access to medical, banking, postal, and other essential services; availability of communications, transportation, and markets; different housing options and living arrangements; and other Volunteer support needs.

You will also learn about Peace Corps/Tanzania's **detailed emergency action plan**, which is implemented in the event of civil or political unrest or a natural disaster. When you arrive at your site, you will complete and submit a site locator form with your address, contact information, and a map to your house. If there is a security threat, you will gather with other Volunteers in Tanzania at predetermined locations until the situation is resolved or the Peace Corps decides to evacuate.

Finally, in order for the Peace Corps to be fully responsive to the needs of Volunteers, it is imperative that Volunteers immediately report any security incident to the Peace Corps office. The Peace Corps has established protocols for **addressing safety and security incidents** in a timely and appropriate manner, and it collects and evaluates safety and security data to track trends and develop strategies to minimize risks to future Volunteers.

DIVERSITY AND CROSS-CULTURAL ISSUES

In fulfilling its mandate to share the face of America with host countries, the Peace Corps is making special efforts to assure that all of America's richness is reflected in the Volunteer corps. More Americans of color are serving in today's Peace Corps than at any time in recent history. Differences in race, ethnic background, age, religion, and sexual orientation are expected and welcomed among our Volunteers. Part of the Peace Corps' mission is to help dispel any notion that Americans are all of one origin or race and to establish that each of us is as thoroughly American as the other despite our many differences.

Our diversity helps us accomplish that goal. In other ways, however, it poses challenges. In Tanzania, as in other Peace Corps host countries, Volunteers' behavior, lifestyle, background, and beliefs are judged in a cultural context very different from their own. Certain personal perspectives or characteristics commonly accepted in the United States may be quite uncommon, unacceptable, or even repressed in Tanzania.

Outside of Tanzania's capital, residents of rural communities have had relatively little direct exposure to other cultures, races, religions, and lifestyles. What people view as typical American behavior or norms may be a misconception, such as the belief that all Americans are rich and have blond hair and blue eyes. The people of Tanzania are justly known for their generous hospitality to foreigners; however, members of the community in which you will live may display a range of reactions to cultural differences that you present.

To ease the transition and adapt to life in Tanzania, you may need to make some temporary, yet fundamental compromises in how you present yourself as an American and as an individual. For example, female trainees and Volunteers may not be able to exercise the independence available to them in the United States; political discussions need to be handled with great care; and some of your personal beliefs may best remain undisclosed. You will need to develop techniques and personal strategies for coping with these and other limitations. The Peace Corps staff will lead diversity and sensitivity discussions during pre-service training and will be on call to provide support, but the challenge ultimately will be your own.

Overview of Diversity in Tanzania

The Peace Corps staff in Tanzania recognizes the adjustment issues that come with diversity and will endeavor to provide support and guidance. During pre-service training, several sessions will be held to discuss diversity and coping mechanisms. We look forward to having male and female Volunteers from a variety of races, ethnic groups, ages, religions, and sexual orientations, and hope that you will become part of a diverse group of Americans who take pride in supporting one another and demonstrating the richness of American culture.

What Might a Volunteer Face?

Possible Issues for Female Volunteers

The notion of gender equality, as Americans understand it, has been slow to take hold in Tanzania. As an American woman, however, you may be viewed as having a higher status than a Tanzanian woman. You could view this as frustrating, or you could see it as an opportunity to help change people's views. It is possible to become a role model — if Tanzanian women see another woman being given respect and functioning in a position of authority, they may be inspired to seek the same.

Of course, American women may also be treated the same way Tanzanian women are. In Tanzanian culture, a man is considered the head of the household — he speaks for the other members. A woman who seems to have knowledge, skills, ideas, and opinions may be viewed as pushy or out of place, or may simply not be taken seriously. Volunteers have to develop their own strategies for addressing this challenge with sensitivity.

"Being a female Volunteer in Tanzania brings additional challenges and unexpected benefits. The challenges come from dealing with assumptions made about you that have nothing to do with your abilities. One benefit is being accepted, no questions asked, into a very warm and supportive female subculture at site. You're dealing with a different set of rules here, but that's not without positive aspects."

"Sometimes it is very difficult being a female Volunteer in Tanzania. There are many cultural expectations that people have of women. But in my time in Tanzania, my female friends have taught me something, and I have taught them, too. I have begun to understand exactly what being a woman is in this culture, and in my own. The greatest way a woman can serve in the Peace Corps is to be an example for the children, youth, and adults who are your companions and co-workers. Tanzanians have never forgotten and will never forget a person who changes their lives."

Possible Issues for Volunteers of Color

The average Tanzanian is not exposed to the diversity of people and cultures that exists in America. If you are black, you are likely to be called Mwafrika (African); if you are Asian, Mchina (Chinese); if you are South Asian, Muhindi (Indian), and if you are European or Hispanic, Mzungu (foreigner). Be prepared to tolerate terms that are considered derogatory in America (e.g., "half-caste" or "colored"), an unfortunate part of Western culture that some may have unwittingly adopted.

African Americans are in a unique situation. While Tanzanians may voice their doubt as to whether you are "really American" (i.e., because you are not white, blond, and blue-eyed), you are likely to have an easier time integrating into the local culture than Caucasian Volunteers.

"There are some challenges as an African American Volunteer. The word 'American' to a Tanzanian often means a white person. Hence, my being African American is often translated as being biracial — African (black parent) and American (white parent). I cannot count the number of times I've been asked about being 'mixed' or 'half-caste.' 'Does your mother look like you?' Yes. 'Does your father look like you?' Yes. 'What tribe are they?'

"For me, as an African American Volunteer, going to Africa meant returning home. Instead of noticing all of the differences between Tanzanians and Americans, I was often amazed by all the similarities. The bibi (grandmother) in my community tries to feed me as much as my own grandmother would! The strength in the hands and eyes of my neighbors is the same strength I saw every day growing up. The jokes, laughter, and dancing of the vijana (young people) are mirror reflections of my sisters and brothers back home. Tanzanians may be speaking a different language, but the spirit, beauty, and meaning are the same."

Possible Issues for Senior Volunteers

While Tanzanians generally have great reverence for age, Tanzania's legal retirement age is 60, and there is the perception that those past middle age are getting ready to "rest." Senior Volunteers will automatically be respected for their wisdom, which is a great advantage, but may be seen as oddities, especially since most Peace Corps Volunteers in Tanzania are young. Tanzanians are especially curious about older female Volunteers. They are puzzled as to why they apparently have no spouse or children (even if they have the pictures to prove otherwise) and why they would leave their extended family to volunteer in Africa.

"I was often asked why I had no children. I understood that it was very uncommon for a woman my age to not have children. Tanzanians would joke that they could help me with a husband or give me some dawa, or medicine, that would help me to have kids. The people in my community were curious about these issues, but soon accepted me as I was."

Possible Issues for Married Couple Volunteers

Most Peace Corps Volunteers are single, but some married couples join the Peace Corps together, and in other cases, one spouse stays in the United States. Each of these situations presents its own challenges and rewards.

"My husband and I got married just a few months before we joined the Peace Corps. We were told before we joined that being in the Peace Corps could put a big strain on a relationship, especially in the beginning of a marriage. But we were also told that the Peace Corps could be extremely rewarding for a married couple. We knew we would be glad to have each other there as support. Since we had already been together for many years, we knew we had a good foundation for our relationship, so we felt confident that we would grow closer through this experience. During our first few months at our site, we found this to be more true than we had imagined. The first month, especially, was filled with learning how to adjust to everything — our new house, a new culture, new foods, new ways to cook, new ways to clean, and a new system of transportation (or the lack thereof). During this time, we really depended on each other to keep up our spirits, to make jokes of the frustrations, to keep busy and entertained during the slow times, and to enjoy the full experience with all its ups and downs. We became even closer than we were before. Neither of us could imagine being in Peace Corps without the other."

Possible Issues for Gay, Lesbian, or Bisexual Volunteers

Tanzania is a very conservative society. Some Tanzanians deny that homosexuality exists in their culture, while others note that it is against the law. A law in Zanzibar makes homosexuality illegal, with prison sentences of 8-15 years. Thus, any display of your sexual orientation will be severely frowned upon and may affect your acceptance at work and possibly even your legal status. While physical contact between two men or two women is not uncommon, it is not likely to be sexual in nature and you should not misinterpret its meaning. Previous gay, lesbian, and bisexual Volunteers have had to be very discreet about their orientation to prevent adverse effects on their relationships with their community and co-workers. However, you are likely to find plenty of support and understanding among the Peace Corps staff and other Volunteers.

"Although I feel like I have close friends in my village, my sexual orientation is something I have to hide from them. Homo- or bisexuality is not understood by a majority of Tanzanians, especially those who live outside the big cities. This does not mean that I have ignored this part of my life for two years. Fellow Peace Corps Volunteers and the American staff are extremely supportive."

A recommended resource for support and advice prior to and during your service is the Lesbian, Gay, Bisexual & Transgender U.S. Peace Corps Alumni website at **www.lgbrpcv.org**.

Possible Religious Issues for Volunteers

You are likely to be asked to share in religious observances, whether it is going to church, breaking the fast during Ramadan, burying an elder in a traditional ceremony, or simply giving thanks to God by saying "Namshukuru Mungu" or "Al-ham D'ililah" as part of your morning greetings. You do not have to participate in regular religious services to be a successful Volunteer in Tanzania, but participation in the religious life of your town or village will provide increased credibility and a sense of community for any Volunteer who is so inclined. Religion is deeply ingrained in the culture, which you will notice just by walking down a city street, where signs for churches, mosques, and madarasat (religious schools) and stickers proclaiming thoughts like, "This car is protected by the blood of Jesus!" abound. When meeting someone for the first time, Tanzanians often ask what his or her religion is.

The religious makeup of the country is roughly split into thirds — Muslims, Christians, and traditionalists. Muslims are the predominant group on Zanzibar (i.e., Pemba and Unguja islands) and along the coast because of the influence of Arab traders and the Omani dynasties, which lasted until the 1800s. Christians (largely Roman Catholics, Lutherans, Pentecostals, and Anglicans) predominate in the interior, although Christian missionaries travel and live throughout Tanzania. Traditional religions are practiced mostly in the northern half of the country by seminomadic tribes such as the Masai, Hadza, and Barabaig.

"I have never been prayed for (at least within my earshot) as much as I have been in Tanzania. My record, though, was when I had an accident and spent a week in the hospital. I was prayed for by my roommate's friends (people I didn't even know) no fewer than three times daily. This usually involved waving their hands in the air and speaking very loudly. There was also a woman who just went room to room laying her hands on patients (including me) and speaking in tongues. I got better, so I guess it worked."

"Entering the Peace Corps was part of a very spiritual experience for me. I was placed in a community that was very focused on the church. There were three Christian churches and a strong implied standard for the lives of the villagers. In time, my relationships and involvement with the church became my most valued aspect of life in the village. The personal examples of friends and neighbors and how they continually trusted in God helped me to grow in my beliefs. My involvement with the church also provided me with a foundation for many working relationships that continue to be fruitful today."

Possible Issues for Volunteers With Disabilities

As part of the medical clearance process, the Peace Corps Office of Medical Services determined that you were physically and emotionally capable, with or without reasonable accommodations, to perform a full tour of Volunteer service in Tanzania without unreasonable risk of harm to yourself or interruption of service. The Peace Corps/ Tanzania staff will work with disabled Volunteers to make reasonable accommodations for them in training, housing, jobsites, or other areas to enable them to serve safely and effectively.

Tanzanians with physical disabilities generally are treated no differently from other Tanzanians, but unlike the U.S., there is little of the infrastructure to accommodate individuals with disabilities. That being said, as part of the medical clearance process, the Peace Corps' Office of Medical Services determined that you were physically and emotionally capable, with or without reasonable accommodations, of performing a full tour of Volunteer service in Tanzania without reasonable risk of harm to yourself or interruption of your service. Peace Corps/Tanzania staff will work with disabled Volunteers to make reasonable accommodations in training, housing, job sites, and other areas to enable them to serve safely and effectively.

FREQUENTLY ASKED QUESTIONS

This list has been compiled by Volunteers serving in Tanzania and is based on their experience. Use it as an informal guide in making your own list, bearing in mind that each experience is individual. There is no perfect list! You obviously cannot bring everything on the list, so consider those items that make the most sense to you personally and professionally. You can always have things sent to you later. As you decide what to bring, keep in mind that you have a 100-pound weight limit on baggage. And remember, you can get almost everything you need in Tanzania.

How much luggage am I allowed to bring to Tanzania?

Most airlines have baggage size and weight limits and assess charges for transport of baggage that exceeds those limits. The Peace Corps has its own size and weight limits and will not pay the cost of transport for baggage that exceeds these limits. The Peace Corps' allowance is two checked pieces of luggage with combined dimensions of both pieces not to exceed 107 inches (length + width + height) and a carry-on bag with dimensions of no more than 45 inches. Checked baggage should not exceed 100 pounds total with a maximum weight of 50 pounds for any one bag.

Peace Corps Volunteers are not allowed to take pets, weapons, explosives, radio transmitters (shortwave radios are permitted), automobiles, or motorcycles to their overseas assignments. Do not pack flammable materials or liquids such as lighter fluid, cleaning solvents, hair spray, or aerosol containers. This is an important safety precaution.

What is the electric current in Tanzania?

It is 220 volts, 50 cycles. Approximately half the Volunteers in Tanzania have electricity at work or at home. But the supply is not always steady, especially in the dry season. Batteries are available, but "D" cells are more easily found than "C" cells. Some Volunteers use solar battery chargers for radios and small appliances.

How much money should I bring?

Volunteers are expected to live at the same level as the people in their community. You will be given a settling-in allowance and a monthly living allowance, which should cover your expenses. Volunteers often wish to bring additional money for vacation travel to other countries. Credit cards and traveler's checks are preferable to cash. If you choose to bring extra money, bring the amount that will suit your own travel plans and needs.

When can I take vacation and have people visit me?

Each Volunteer accrues two vacation days per month of service (excluding training). Leave may not be taken during training, the first three months of service, or the last three months of service, except in conjunction with an authorized emergency leave. Family and friends are welcome to visit you after pre-service training and the first three months of service as long as their stay does not interfere with your work. Extended stays at your site are not encouraged and may require permission from your country director. The Peace Corps is not able to provide your visitors with visa, medical, or travel assistance.

Will my belongings be covered by insurance?

The Peace Corps does not provide insurance coverage for personal effects; Volunteers are ultimately responsible for the safekeeping of their personal belongings. However, you can purchase personal property insurance before you leave. If you wish, you may contact your own insurance company; additionally, insurance application forms will be provided, and we encourage you to consider them carefully. Volunteers should not ship or take valuable items overseas. Jewelry, watches, radios, cameras, and expensive appliances are subject to loss, theft, and breakage, and in many places, satisfactory maintenance and repair services are not available.

Do I need an international driver's license?

Volunteers in Tanzania do not need an international driver's license because they are prohibited from operating privately owned motorized vehicles. Most urban travel is by bus or taxi. Rural travel ranges from buses and minibuses to trucks, bicycles, and lots of walking. On very rare occasions, a Volunteer may be asked to drive a sponsor's vehicle, but this can occur only with prior written permission from the country director. Should this occur, the Volunteer may obtain a local driver's license. A U.S. driver's license will facilitate the process, so bring it with you just in case.

What should I bring as gifts for Tanzania friends and my host family?

This is not a requirement. A token of friendship is sufficient. Some gift suggestions include knickknacks for the house; pictures, books, or calendars of American scenes; souvenirs from your area; hard candies that will not melt or spoil; or photos to give away.

Where will my site assignment be when I finish training and how isolated will I be?

Peace Corps trainees are not assigned to individual sites until after they have completed pre-service training. This gives Peace Corps staff the opportunity to assess each trainee's technical and language skills prior to assigning sites, in addition to finalizing site selections with their ministry counterparts. If feasible, you may have the opportunity to provide input on your site preferences, including geographical location, distance from other Volunteers, and living conditions. However, keep in mind that many factors influence the site selection process and that the Peace Corps cannot guarantee placement where you would ideally like to be. Most Volunteers live in small towns or in rural villages and are usually within one hour from another Volunteer. Some sites require a 10- to 12-hour drive from the capital. There is at least one Volunteer based in each of the regional capitals and about five to eight Volunteers in the capital Dar es Salaam.

How can my family contact me in an emergency?

The Peace Corps' Office of Special Services (OSS) provides assistance in handling emergencies affecting trainees and Volunteers or their families. Before leaving the United States, instruct your family to notify the Office of Special Services immediately if an emergency arises, such as a serious illness or death of a family member. During normal business hours, the number for the Office of Special Services is 855.855.1961, then select option 2; or directly at 202-692-1470. After normal business hours and on weekends and holidays, the OSS duty officer can be reached at the above number. For non-emergency questions, your family can get information from your country desk staff at the Peace Corps by calling 855.855.1961.

Can I call home from Tanzania?

International phone service from Tanzania to the United States is poor to good depending on the location. It is easier (and far cheaper) for your family and friends to call you from the United States. However, you are likely to find a phone from which you can call family and friends within a few hours of your site.

Should I bring a cellular phone with me?

Cell phone service is growing in many, but not all, parts of the country. About 90 percent of Volunteers in Tanzania now have cell phones, and the number is growing. Not all Volunteers have network coverage at their sites, but use the phones when they get to a location with coverage. Differences in technology make most U.S. cell phones incompatible with local service, so only phones purchased in Tanzania are likely to work. Cell phones are very readily available in Tanzania.

Will there be email and Internet access? Should I bring my computer?

E-mail and Internet services are available for reasonable fees at cybercafés in all large towns and a growing number of smaller towns. Volunteers also have access to e-mail at the Peace Corps office in Dar es Salaam. Many Volunteers set up a free e-mail account (e.g., Hotmail or Yahoo) that allows them to retrieve and send e-mail from any computer with Internet access. However, many sites are not near large towns, so you may not be able to communicate regularly by e-mail after training.

Deciding whether to bring a computer is difficult, with some Volunteers arguing for and others against bringing a laptop. There may not be a functioning computer or printer at your school. Many sites, and certainly all environment Volunteer sites, are in rural areas with no, limited, or sporadic electricity. If you decide to bring a computer, you should insure it and expect humidity, fluctuating current, and limited resources for repairs and replacement parts.

WELCOME LETTERS FROM COUNTRY VOLUNTEERS

Getting Started: Training

Most trainees arrive at training vaguely aware of how much they have to learn: a new language, how to fit into a new culture, how to stay healthy on a continent of new and different microbes, and how to accomplish their primary assignments effectively. Ten weeks is shorter than a college semester, and even with nine-hour days, there is a lot to cover. Prepare to be pulled in about six directions at a time until you are sworn in as a Volunteer. Training is a chance to become competent in a lot of different areas, to get your feet wet in a safe and supportive learning environment, and to meet people who are frighteningly similar to you and all the more likable for it. Few Volunteers would say training was their favorite part of the Peace Corps, but I think everyone realizes how impossible the rest of their job would have been without it.

— Peace Corps Volunteer

I'd like to offer you the opportunity to juxtapose your mental states for a while. On the one hand, be prepared to experience new things and new ideas that are beyond what you ever would have expected in "Africa." On the other hand, know that it is all about people and those people, no matter where you are, are still full of the same creative energy, dreams, and longings. It will all be new to you, and nothing at all will be new. What matters is that you are ready for this paradox, which isn't really a paradox, by coming to Tanzania with open minds and open hearts. It may hurt a bit at first, but it will change you and shape you forever.

— Peace Corps Volunteer

Working in Tanzania

Your work here in Tanzania will prove to be some of the most challenging and frustrating — but at the same time some of the most beneficial and rewarding — work you may ever do in your life. The village working environment is very different from working environments in the Western world. Here, people are working to live; that is to say, they are working to produce the food they and their families need to survive. And this commitment to survival plays an important role in making decisions and getting involved in various projects.

Karibu Tanzania! Let us introduce ourselves — we are the Volunteer Advisory Committee for Peace Corps/Tanzania, made up of Volunteers from different regions in Tanzania. We work with the office in Dar es Salaam and also with Volunteers to make Volunteer life as smooth and as rewarding as possible. It's in that regard that we would like to offer a friendly reminder — clothing counts!

How does it count? It is the first and last thing Tanzanians will consider when formulating their opinions about you. And since you'll be working with them for two (or more) years, you will want that opinion to be positive from the beginning. It may seem a trivial thing, but it will earn you credibility points galore in your village or town. You may have already read the clothing packing list, but we want to reiterate to you that proper attire is necessary for success in the field.

Good luck and we look forward to meeting you!

— Volunteer Advisory Committee

Daily Life

So after months and possibly years of medical examinations and background checks, you've finally received your invitation to join us in Tanzania. Congratulations! You don't know this now, but by sheer luck you've pulled the best location in Africa and arguably the world. Tanzania offers so many things to Peace Corps Volunteers. From the outset you will find the people of East Africa to be engaging and the lifestyle to be laid-back and peaceful. Tanzania exemplifies the melting pot of East African culture. With so many tribes, customs, cultures, traditions, and local languages, you're apt to feel overwhelmed by the amount of rich history located here. Don't be!

Time here operates six hours behind schedule, literally. Your adjustment process will be entirely up to you and your willingness to embrace the culture. The Peace Corps is a funny thing. The challenges and obstacles you're preparing for right now will not be the ones with which you struggle. Right now you're probably worried about packing, fitting in, learning the language, and so on. You will find that these problems dwarf rather quickly in comparison. The real challenges will be whether you eat beans and rice or rice and beans. Whether the customs agent will charge you your entire living allowance to get that package your mom sent you, even though you live in the desert. Whether you'll be able to fight your way out of the mosquito net in time to get to the bathroom, conveniently located one-half kilometer from your house. These are the real issues, and no amount of contemplation and research will prepare you for the type of decisions you will need to make. That's exciting.

Do yourself a favor. Relax. Sit back these next few months and spend time with your family, friends, and loved ones. Your new family is here. We are waiting for you and preparing every day for your arrival. You will be taken care of. This can be a very exciting time in your life. Take the initiative to make it that way.

— Joe Dupelle

Greetings Peace Corps Trainees!

Karibu! Welcome to Tanzania, the jewel of Africa; the home of Zanzibar, Mount Kilimanjaro, 14 national parks, extremely friendly people, and your new home! I hope all your paperwork and red tape experiences are behind you. Now your real adventure is about to begin. You've made it this far and only have a little further to go.

I am an environmental Volunteer doing community-based natural resource management. I live in the southern highlands of Tanzania, a short 10- to 11-hour bus ride from the amazing city of Dar Es Salaam. My village name is Idindilimunyo (e-dee-knee-dee-lee-moon-yo), in the Njombe district, Iringa region. I live on a two-acre plot of land, my farm, about 75 meters from the local primary school. Life in the village is great and humbling to say the least.

As an environmental Volunteer, I have a broad range of areas in which to help the local villagers. Currently, I am extending a water pipe 2.5 km to a sub-village that will provide more than 360 people with fresh running water. I work with another Volunteer on health issues in the village, mainly pertaining to maternal and paternal healthcare. I've taught about making food for weaning babies, sanitation issues, pit latrine construction, and nutritional needs for pregnant women. I have worked with primary school students planting banana trees, helped women's groups start income-generating activities, brought villagers to an agriculture festival to learn new agriculture and livestock skills, introduced improved sunflower and maize seeds, and taught contouring techniques to reduce soil erosion. As I'm doing all this, I'm hopefully creating a positive, long-lasting image of Americans.

I feel very fortunate to live and work here. It has far exceeded my expectations on all levels. The highs are higher than I've ever been and the same goes with the lows. Life here doesn't occur without difficulties, as you are away from everything you know and living in a developing country. Fortunately you are not alone. Fellow Volunteers will be there to support you, along with the amazing Peace Corps/Tanzania staff.

As you are saying goodbye to all your loved ones, know that you are about to begin two of the most unforgettable years of your life. I awake every day in awe of the life I am leading. I've made friends I'll never lose touch with; had experiences no book, television show, or lecture could teach; and touched more lives than I ever expected. I hope your plane trip over will be memorable. Don't forget to buy your favorite magazine(s) while at the Amsterdam Airport; it's the last one you'll be seeing for a while. I look forward to meeting you and good luck in training.

Cheers and Peace,

— Scott J Pietka

Welcome to Tanzania! I am a second-year information technology Volunteer in Bukoba, up on the western shore of Lake Victoria. You should feel quite lucky to have been placed in Tanzania. The Peace Corps community is large, supportive, and energetic, and your host families and host communities will likely make you uncomfortable with their energy and enthusiasm to receive you. This country is a beautiful place to live, but you'll have to discover that for yourselves.

For most of my service, I have been at Ihungo Secondary School, where I teach computer studies to 10 classes in both A and O levels and about anyone else who is interested as well. I also maintain our computer laboratory of about 20 machines and help a few other area schools and organizations maintain their laboratories. The best part about life here, however, is interacting with students on a day-to-day basis. They continue to challenge me, entertain me, encourage me, and surprise me with something new every day. Some of the best moments have been laying around the grass outside when electricity is cut, talking about how to date someone in Tanzania versus America, exploring the world via pictures and videos on our encyclopedia CD-ROM, or just giving them a Nalgene bottle and an ultimatum to break it. (Everyone should try that last one!)

You should know that Tanzanians laugh a lot: at you, at themselves, at everything. You might get embarrassed having people laugh at you constantly as you learn a new language and culture, but after two years I can honestly say they are laughing with you and more out of happiness and surprise that you're speaking their language than out of any mistake you have made. In fact, if you really want to hear people burst out with laughter, greet them in their tribal language! Grow accustomed to the culture of laughing and you'll have a wonderful two years (or more!).

I remember one thing my host family always said to me was, "Kuwa huru (be free)." This could not be better advice; the happiest Volunteers are those who have learned the new culture and language and yet remained true to themselves. Furthermore, I would add, "Kuwa wazi (be open)." If you can manage to be open and free with the Tanzanians you meet, you'll adjust quickly, make many friends, learn more than you can imagine about Africa and yourself, and have a wonderful experience here.

I have been surprised again and again how accepting and friendly my communities have been. I'm a little jealous that you're just starting your service as I am finishing mine, but nonetheless, Karibuni sana! Laugh, be open, and be free.

— Joseph Holler

Dear Invitees,

It wasn't so long ago I was in your shoes; filled with a thousand emotions and questions about my upcoming Tanzanian Peace Corps experience. It seems as though I just blinked and now here I am, one year into service, another year to go. So you may be asking yourself, "What am I in for?" The truth is, no one really knows, because every Volunteer's experience is unique, but I will try to paint my picture to at least give you an idea …

I feel so fortunate to have been assigned to TZ. As you will soon see, it is an amazing country. In many ways, it is the epitome of Africa. When people think of Africa, what comes to mind? Perhaps herds of wild, exotic animals migrating across the Serengeti? Or Mount Kilimanjaro towering over quiet little villages filled with mud huts? Or maybe white, sandy beaches smoothed by a bright turquoise sea? TZ has got it all! Three things TZ has in abundance are: a variety of landscapes, hospitality, and peace. The latter is of particular importance since that may not be one of the things that come to mind when thinking of Africa. But TZ, thankfully, is a peaceful country.

As a community health educator, my main goal is to provide HIV/AIDS education to community members. This means I have the freedom to work with students and teachers, health workers, government employees, out-of-school youth groups, people living with HIV/AIDS (PLWHAs) support groups, community theater/arts groups, or any other groups of people who are interested and in need of education. I am stationed in the community development office at the district government level where I receive guidance on which community groups should be reached and in which way (seminars, literature, theater performances, etc.) in the town of Ifakara.

The house I live in has three small bedrooms, a living room, kitchen and pantry, a shower room, and a toilet room. (Western toilet, not a pit latrine, but be prepared to become well-acquainted with the pit latrine, as they are common. No worries, though. They're not as scary as you think.) My house has electricity and indoor plumbing, although the water pressure is only strong enough to pump water for just a few hours every morning. So I take that time to fill several large buckets that I use as my water source throughout the day. Cooking is done over a charcoal or kerosene stove. I was lucky enough to inherit a small refrigerator from a former Volunteer. Overall, life is more comfortable than I expected it to be. You quickly form routines and get used to your new surroundings. Believe it or not, you may actually grow to prefer your slightly warmed bucket-bath over the cold shower some day!

I truly enjoy being a Peace Corps Volunteer. Most days I welcome the unpredictable challenges and everyday absurdities (like the 30 people crammed into a 10-seat daladala [mini bus] or the live chickens strutting around in the office). But there are, of course, days when I long to go home and feel "normal" again. But then again, what fun is that? So I get through those moments by visiting or text messaging other Volunteers or talking to family at home on my cell phone. (That's right; cell phones are an affordable and reliable means of communication here in TZ!)

The only advice I can offer is this: Hold on to your sense of humor with both hands. Laugh and smile often; it will take you far. Don't let annoyances or failures get you down or make you forget why you decided to do this in the first place. Keep in mind you are growing in more ways than you can imagine, and growing sometimes hurts while you're in the middle of it. But in the end, it'll be so worth it.

So take a quick look at those shoes you're wearing; the ones that I once stood in, because they're about to change. Not just from the layer of red dust they're sure to accumulate within a week of your arrival, but soon they're going to travel to places few people in this world have ever heard of and they are going to experience adventures few people are brave enough to try. Congratulations on your TZ assignment and welcome to the Peace Corps family!

Karibuni sana,

— Katie Reilly

Some people see the glass as half full or half empty. A Peace Corps/Tanzania Volunteer looks at the glass and says, "Gee, I can take a bath in that."

— Peace Corps Volunteer

There comes a time when you realize that resources are not essential and that culture must be embraced and not judged. Then you begin to work on the important issues that you can really do something about and that mean the most to you. It is so easy to fall back on the headaches, but I'm here to share ideas, not to change culture or people. I am here to give tools so others can change their own outlook. And with that always in the back of my mind, I have found I can continually stay positive, hopeful, and energetic.

— Bill Lamonte

PACKING LIST

This list has been compiled by Volunteers serving in Tanzania and is based on their experience. Use it as an informal guide in making your own list, bearing in mind that each experience is individual. There is no perfect list! You obviously cannot bring everything on the list, so consider those items that make the most sense to you personally and professionally. You can always have things sent to you later. As you decide what to bring, keep in mind that you have an 100-pound weight limit on baggage. And remember, you can get almost everything you need in Tanzania.

There are numerous used clothes markets throughout Tanzania where you can purchase inexpensive clothing. Tailors can also make clothing for you. It is possible in the early weeks of training to buy most clothing you will need or to expand on what you have brought. Think of East Africa as the world's largest thrift store; the clothing will all be familiar to you. Once at site, you can pick up quality used clothing at markets that are adequate for your service. Clothing found at markets generally range from $1-$5 for an article of clothing. In addition, clothes in Tanzania are hand washed, hung dry and ironed. Therefore, cotton items generally tend to stretch out over time and some materials are not durable enough to endure hand washing.

General Clothing

For Women

- Three to five cotton or polyester dresses or skirts (below the knee or longer).

- Two or three blouses or dressy shirts (no bare shoulders)

- One extra-nice dress for official functions (no bare shoulders, below the knees)

- Socks* (Tanzanian women generally do not wear pantyhose. White gets dirty quickly and cotton does not dry well.)

- Two-year supply of underwear* (For women: bras and slips)

- One pair of lightweight, quick-drying ankle pants for travel and when riding a bike or exercising

- Five or six short-sleeved T-shirts

For Men

- Three-to-five cotton or synthetic, dark-colored dress or casual pants

- Six or seven button-down shirts (mix of short and long sleeved)

- Two-year supply of underwear* and socks*

- Three short-sleeved T-shirts

- Two pairs of lightweight, quick-drying pants for travel, bike riding, and exercise

- One jacket and tie for official functions (you will use these)

- One or two pairs of shorts

**Many common clothes items can be bought cheaply in country. Pants, tee-shirts and some shoes can be found in all large banking towns. You will need a few articles of clothing for the first few months of training before you go to your banking town.

Shoes

- One pair of nice but comfortable shoes (to wear with professional clothes)

- Durable walking shoes or hiking boots*

- Sandals, e.g. Teva* brand or Chacos* brand. Strongly recommended (a must for environment Volunteers). Inquire on websites about Peace Corps Volunteer discounts.

- One pair of sneakers or running shoes

- Closed-toe shoes or dressy sandals

Note: hiking boots are only necessary if you're going to be doing a lot of mountain climbing. Even then, fairly high-quality used boots are available in-country. Your best bet may be to buy a decent pair of tennis shoes which will be more than adequate 99 percent of the time. Also, flip-flops are available in abundance; don't bring any!

Personal Hygiene and Toiletry Items

Most toiletries are readily available in Tanzania, but you may not find your favorite brand. Deodorant is in limited supply in Tanzania. Hairbrushes or toothbrushes are available in shops at different quality and certain items will be comparatively expensive. Women should bring tampons or a diva cup.

Kitchen

Most household items are readily available. If you like to cook, consider bringing some of the following items, or mail them to yourself.

- Plastic Ziploc storage bags of various sizes (a must to keep out unwanted crawling critters)*

- Good kitchen knife*

- Mexican or your favorite, unique spices* (most other spices are available especially Italian and Indian spices)

- Various powdered mixes (e.g., soft-drink mixes, salad dressings, soups, and sauce packets)

- Vegetable Peeler

Entertainment

Volunteers often have downtime, so bringing some of the items suggested below can make a difference. But remember that most rural areas do not have electricity. Consider bringing a good supply of batteries, especially solar-powered batteries or rechargeable batteries and a charger. Please note that in Tanzania the electricity that is used is 220V.

- Ipod or Kindle
- Shortwave radio
- Digital Camera
- Binoculars
- Musical instruments (plus extra strings, reeds, etc.)
- Sport, hobby, and art equipment and supplies
- Games (e.g., cards, dice, hacky sack, yo-yos, Frisbee, juggling balls, dominoes)
- Camping gear (tent, backpack, sleeping pad, etc.), if you are interested in camping
- Books
- How-to-books (for working with kids)

Miscellaneous

- A small current converter (if you bring small appliances like a shaver, etc.)
- English dictionary and/or thesaurus
- Multi-purpose knife (e.g., Swiss Army knife, Leatherman or Gerber; a must for environment Volunteers)
- Flashlight/headlamp and batteries (Note that AAA batteries are hard to come by)
- A solar battery charger and rechargeable batteries
- A small amount of seeds to plant, especially herbs for the garden
- Combination padlocks of various sizes (good key locks can be found in-country)
- Sewing kit
- Photos of your home and family (your neighbors will love them)
- Sturdy water bottle (e.g., Nalgene)
- Money belt (critical for traveling on public transport)
- Travel alarm clock
- Duct or packing tape

- Day pack

- Hand held UV water sterilizer (good for traveling, make sure you have quality batteries)

- Journal or diary

- Fly swatter (they can be irritating)

- Visa Debit Card (easiest way to access emergency money from home)

- USB drive or larger portable hard drive

PRE-DEPARTURE CHECKLIST

The following list consists of suggestions for you to consider as you prepare to live outside the United States for two years. Not all items will be relevant to everyone, and the list does not include everything you should make arrangements for.

Family

- Notify family that they can call the Peace Corps' Counseling and Outreach Unit at any time if there is a critical illness or death of a family member (24-hour telephone number: 1-855-855-1961, then press 2; or directly at 202-692-1470).

- Give the Peace Corps' On the Home Front handbook to family and friends.

Passport/Travel

- Forward to the Peace Corps travel office all paperwork for the Peace Corps passport and visas.

- Verify that your luggage meets the size and weight limits for international travel.

- Obtain a personal passport if you plan to travel after your service ends. (Your Peace Corps passport will expire three months after you finish your service, so if you plan to travel longer, you will need a regular passport.)

Medical/Health

- Complete any needed dental and medical work.

- If you wear glasses, bring two pairs.

- Arrange to bring a three-month supply of all medications (including birth control pills) you are currently taking.

Insurance

- Make arrangements to maintain life insurance coverage.

- Arrange to maintain supplemental health coverage while you are away. (Even though the Peace Corps is responsible for your health care during Peace Corps service overseas, it is advisable for people who have pre-existing conditions to arrange for the continuation of their supplemental health coverage. If there is a lapse in coverage, it is often difficult and expensive to be reinstated.)

- Arrange to continue Medicare coverage if applicable.

Personal Papers

- Bring a copy of your certificate of marriage or divorce.

Voting

- Register to vote in the state of your home of record. (Many state universities consider voting and payment of state taxes as evidence of residence in that state.)

- Obtain a voter registration card and take it with you overseas.

- Arrange to have an absentee ballot forwarded to you overseas.

Personal Effects

- Purchase personal property insurance to extend from the time you leave your home for service overseas until the time you complete your service and return to the United States.

Financial Management

- Keep a bank account in your name in the U.S.

- Obtain student loan deferment forms from the lender or loan service.

- Execute a Power of Attorney for the management of your property and business.

- Arrange for deductions from your readjustment allowance to pay alimony, child support, and other debts through the Office of Volunteer Financial Operations at 855.855.1961, extension 1770.

- Place all important papers—mortgages, deeds, stocks, and bonds—in a safe deposit box or with an attorney or other caretaker.

CONTACTING PEACE CORPS HEADQUARTERS

This list of numbers will help connect you with the appropriate office at Peace Corps headquarters to answer various questions. You can use the toll-free number and extension or dial directly using the local numbers provided. Be sure to leave the toll-free number and extensions with your family so they can contact you in the event of an emergency.

Peace Corps Headquarters Toll-free Number: 855.855.1961, Press 1 or ext. # (see below)

Peace Corps' Mailing Address:

Peace Corps Headquarters
1111 20th Street, NW
Washington, DC 20526

Questions About:	Staff:	Toll-Free Ext:	Direct/Local #:
Responding to an Invitation	Office of Placement	x1840	202.692.1840
Country Information	Kelly Daly Desk Officer / (Tanzania & Madagascar) Tanzania@peacecorps.gov	X2366	202.692.2366
Plane Tickets, Passports, Visas, or other travel matters:	CWT SATO Travel	x1170	202.692.1170
Legal Clearance	Office of Placement	x1840	202.692.1840
Medical Clearance & Forms Processing (includes dental)	Screening Nurse	x1500	202.692.1500
Medical Reimbursements (handled by a subcontractor)	Seven Corners	N/A	202.692.1538 800.335.0611
Loan Deferments, Taxes, Financial Operations	Office Of Volunteer and PSC Financial Services	x1770	202.692.1770
Readjustment Allowance Withdrawals, Power of Attorney, Staging (Pre-Departure Orientation), and Reporting Instructions	Office of Staging *Note: You will receive comprehensive information (hotel and flight arrangements) three to five weeks prior to departure. This information is not available sooner.*	x1865	202.692.1865
Family Emergencies (to get information to a Volunteer overseas) 24 hours	Office of Special Services	x1470	202.692.1470

Made in the USA
Monee, IL
04 January 2025

76094936R10031